AH MO

AH MO

Indian Legends from
the Northwest

Compiled by Judge Arthur Griffin
Edited by Trenholme J. Griffin
Illustrated by Margaret Chodos-Irvine

hancock
house

ISBN 0-88839-244-3
Copyright © 1990 Trenholme James Griffin

Fourth printing 2004

Cataloging in Publication Data
Griffin, Trenholme James, 1955–
    Ah mo
    Indian legends from the northwest

    Includes biographical references.
    ISBN 0-88839-244-3

    1. Indians of North America—Washington (State)—Legends.
I. Title.
E78.W3G75 1990   398.2'089970797   C90-091109-3

Editor/Designer: Herb Bryce
Production: Lorna Lake
Production Assistant: Cheryl Smyley

Compiled by Judge Arthur Griffin
Illustrated by Margaret Chodos-Irvine

Published simultaneously in Canada and the United States by

HANCOCK HOUSE PUBLISHERS LTD.
19313 Zero Avenue, Surrey, B.C. V3S 9R9
(604) 538-1114 Fax (604) 538-2262

HANCOCK HOUSE PUBLISHERS
1431 Harrison Avenue, Blaine, WA 98230-5005
(604) 538-1114 Fax (604) 538-2262
Web Site: www.hancockhouse.com *Email:* sales@hancockhouse.com

Your religion was written upon tables of stone by the iron finger of your God so that you could not forget. The Red Man could never comprehend nor remember it. Our religion is the traditions of our ancestors—the dreams of our old men, given them in solemn hours of night by the Great Spirit; and the visions of our sachems; and it is written in the hearts of our people.

CHIEF SEALTH

To Nancy
For her inspiration and support.

Contents

Acknowledgments 8
Introduction 9
1   The Loon 12
    A Twana Legend
2   The Gossiping Clams 14
    A Suquamish Legend
3   The Blackberry .16
    A Snohomish Legend
4   The Octopus 18
    A Lummi Legend
5   Why Rivers Have Bends 22
    A Chinook Legend
6   Days and Nights 24
    A Kittitas Legend
7   Why the Crane Has Long Legs 28
    A Puyallup Legend
8   The Sun and the Moon 32
    A Snoqualmie Legend
9   Why the Robin Has a Red Breast 36
    A Suquamish Legend
10 The Coyote 40
    A Kittitas Legend
11 The Fish Duck and the Sea Gull 44
    A Skagit Legend
12 The North Wind 48
    A Snoqualmie Legend
13 How the Indians Obtained Fire 54
    A Snoqualmie Legend
    Judge Arthur E. Griffin 58
    Museums with Significant Collections 63
    Suggested Reading List 64

Ah Mo would have not been possible without the editorial assistance of Nancy Griffin, the writing and compilation work of Dr. Tren Griffin and my friends at Preston Thorgrimson Shidler Gates and Ellis.

Introduction

This book contains legends collected by Judge Arthur E. Griffin from Indian tribes in Washington State. The legends were told to Judge Griffin by Indian storytellers between 1884 and 1947. The legends have been rewritten by the Judge's grandson and great-grandson to make them more pleasant for children to read. Serious students of Indian folklore should refer to the original stories which reflect the complex writing style of the period. The original stories collected by Judge Griffin can be found in research libraries, such as Suzzallo Library at the University of Washington.

Indian storytellers were skilled at bringing each of the characters and animals in the legend to life through gestures and animal calls. Since the storytellers lived with the birds, fish and animals, few secrets were hidden from their keen vision. The legends were told in the lights and shadows around open fires, which gave the stories a magical quality.

Some of the Indian storytellers were professionals who traveled from village to village. The Indian children were required to pay strict attention when a story was being told. To prove they were listening, the children were told to say "Ah Mo" at frequent intervals. As the "Ah Mos" diminished, the children were whisked off to bed.

The legends in this book took place a time long ago when people, animals, and forces of nature could talk to each other. People and animals often had magical powers to do what would be impossible today. Spiders could climb into the sky and a boy could turn himself into the sun. The Indians referred to this time as having been "before the change." The Indians also believed that every person and animal had a guardian spirit who protected and watched over them. The guardian spirit usually took the form of an animal and had magical powers which allowed people and animals to escape danger and perform heroic deeds. Young Indian men ventured alone into the forest, hoping for a sign informing them which animal was their guardian spirit. Chief Sealth, the man who gave the city of Seattle its name, discovered as a young man that his guardian spirit was a sea gull.

1

TheLoon

A Twana Legend

A long time ago, there were no loons. The story of how these loons came to this world is sad but true. One day a young Indian girl and her twin brother were playing in the shallow water of Hood Canal while their mother was digging for clams on the shore. The children were only seven years old and had been told many times to stay close to the shore. But they were very fond of swimming and diving and soon moved to deeper and deeper water. The mother saw the children straying and called for them to return to the shore. The young boy and girl laughed at her and swam to still deeper water. The mother became frightened and began to cry. The children laughed even harder and began to mimic her calls for them to return to shore.

As their mother sat crying because the children would not return to shallow water, the Great Spirit appeared at the beach. He saw the children swimming in the deep water and heard them mock their mother. To punish the children, the Great Spirit used his great powers to turn them into loons. To this day, you can hear the long, lonesome cries this bird makes as it remembers the day the Indian children disobeyed their mother.

● ● ●

2

The Gossiping Clams

A Suquamish Legend

A long time ago, clams were great gossipers. The other animals believed the clams talked so much because their mouths stretched the full length of their bodies. The gossiping of the clams often caused severe trouble for the other animals.

Raven finally became so tired of the gossiping that he called a council meeting. Each of the animals agreed that, in order to preserve peace, a way must be found to stop the gossiping of the clams. After much discussion, the animals chose Beaver to find a solution to the problem.

After many weeks of thinking, Beaver came up with a plan. He gathered all of the clams in his arms and took them to the beach, where the tide flows in and out twice a day. Beaver then buried the clams deep in the sand so that every time a clam opened its mouth, sand and water would rush into it.

To this day, if you walk along the beach when the tide is out, you will notice little streams of water spurting from the sand. Don't be alarmed. It's only the clams spitting out the sand and water they swallow when they try to gossip.

•   •   •

3

The Blackberry

A Snohomish Legend

A long time ago, Blackberry was an upright tree which grew as tall as the other trees in the forest. It had long branches and sharp thorns. Blackberry had always lived at peace with the animals and was very popular.

For a reason known only to the Great Spirit, the attitude of Blackberry changed from friendly to hostile. Blackberry began to throw his long branches around any animal which came within his reach. He would then hold the poor animal with his thorns until it died. Blackberry grew taller and stronger as the ground became enriched with the bones of the animals he had trapped and killed.

The animals complained to Spelyi, the wolf, about the evil ways of Blackberry. Spelyi did not hesitate in responding to this problem. He grabbed a heavy club and climbed up a tall fir tree which grew near Blackberry. Spelyi then walked out on a limb and smashed Blackberry until every one of his branches had fallen to the ground. Since that day, Blackberry has been a bush rather than a tree.

That is why you will find the blackberry growing low to the ground, where it is so weak it can no longer harm animals by catching them in its branches and holding them with its thorns.

• • •

4

The Octopus

A Lummi Legend

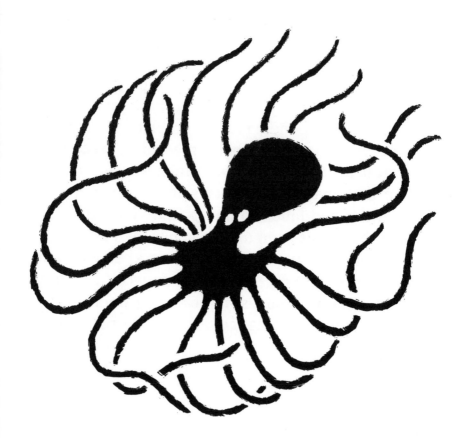

A long time ago, Octopus had twenty long arms. Octopus could swim very fast and grew to be large and powerful from eating many kinds of fish. He also feasted on animals who came to the shore to eat seaweed in wintertime when the ground was covered with snow. Octopus eventually became so strong and bold that he began to attack Indians in their canoes.

One day an Indian chief named Siam decided to go fishing in his canoe. Siam was athletic and very strong. He had been selected as chief of the tribe for his strength as well as his courage in fighting the northern Indians who traveled to Puget Sound in their great war canoes to capture slaves.

Without warning, Octopus attacked the canoe and wound his arms around the Indian chief. Siam struggled to release himself from Octopus, but had no weapon to defend himself. Octopus wrapped each of his twenty arms around Siam and pulled him toward the rocky bottom. Siam was helpless, but fortunately he had taken a deep breath of air before being pulled under the water.

Siam's guardian spirit saw the struggle and decided to help. He found a sharp stone knife, swam to where Octopus and Siam were fighting, and placed the weapon in Siam's right hand. Siam quickly used the knife to cut off one of the long arms of Octopus.

"How can you hope to escape by cutting off only one of my arms?" demanded Octopus, who could talk under water.

Siam knew better than to try to talk and, instead, cut off the arm which Octopus used to hold himself fast to a big rock on the bottom. Siam and Octopus then floated to the surface and Siam took in all the air his lungs would hold.

Octopus soon regained his strength and pulled Siam below again. He then decided to use a trick he used against fish that were his enemies. Octopus expelled a great amount of black fluid. This made the water so black that Siam could not see. Although he was blinded, Siam bravely continued to slash the knife at Octopus. Whenever Octopus wound an arm around Siam's neck to choke him, he cut it off. After Siam had cut off all but nine of the arms, Octopus pleaded, "If you don't cut off any more of my arms, I will let you go."

Siam refused and again cut off the arm Octopus was using to hold them to the bottom. Siam and Octopus then floated to the surface again.

"Now that we are at the surface, I can talk," said Siam. "I will not cut off any more of your arms if you promise not to tip over our canoes."

"I agree," replied Octopus, cleverly saying nothing about harming Indians while they were swimming. Octopus then quickly swam to a deep and dark place. To this day, Octopus is never seen where there is plenty of sunlight.

Siam grabbed two of the severed arms of Octopus, righted his canoe, and paddled home. From the two arms of Octopus, Siam made two ravens. The ravens were very popular with the Indians who lived in the San Juan Islands because they always gave a warning when storms were approaching. They also warned the Indians when war parties from northern tribes were approaching. This allowed Siam's tribe to defeat their enemies in battle.

While Octopus continues to keep his promise to Siam not to overturn canoes, Indian children who have heard this story never swim in places where an octopus might have his home.

• • •

5

Why Rivers Have Bends

A Chinook Legend

A long time ago, Raven wanted the rivers to have bends so that when flying overhead he would have a different view at each bend. Mink disagreed with Raven and wanted the rivers to be straight. This would make it much easier for Mink to follow the banks of the river when he was hunting for frogs. Mink also knew that if the rivers were straight, they would be shorter. This would mean he would be less tired at the end of each day.

Raven and Mink called a council meeting of all the animals to decide how the rivers should run from the mountains to the sea. At the meeting, many arguments were made on both sides of the question. Mink was clever, but he was not clever enough. Because of his loud and persistent voice, Raven and his friends won the argument. To this day, the rivers have bends from the mountains to the sea.

• • •

6

Days and Nights

A Kittitas Legend

A long time ago, before the Great Spirit brought people to this world, a dispute arose among the animals about how long the days and nights should be. The animals that wanted short days and short nights elected Frog as their leader. Bear was chosen by the animals who wanted only one long day and one long night each year. The arguments continued for months and months until both sides agreed to hold an election to decide the issue.

Frog adopted the slogan "Che che twi lich, de de twi lich," which means "Come twilight, go twilight."

Bear chose the slogan "Ba la cha, da la cheil," which means "Long day, long night."

The two sides argued for many hours. Frog grew more stubborn and Bear more angry as each minute passed. Finally, Bear lost his temper and growled at Frog, "I'll eat you alive."

"Catch me first," answered Frog.

Bear tried to crush Frog with a blow from its huge paw but missed. Frog was too quick for Bear and jumped into a nearby pond. Frog swam to the bottom and covered himself with mud. Bear looked and looked for Frog but could not find him. Bear eventually became tired and agreed that the days could last for twelve hours and the nights the same if he and his friends could have a long sleep during the cold winter and Frog would wake them up in the spring. This is why the animals named the month of February "Wauk Waukus," after the sound made by Frog in the spring. To this day, you will never find a bear taking his long winter sleep so far away from a pond that the voices of the frogs will not wake him up in the spring when the weather begins to warm.

•   •   •

AH MO . . .

7

Why the Crane Has Long Legs

A Puyallup Legend

A long time ago, Crane was known by all the animals as a great fisherman, although he was only able to fish in shallow water. Little Diver was also skilled at catching fish, but did all her fishing in deep water. Crane admired Little Diver, both for her fishing ability and for her slim, glossy, and graceful neck. Crane fell in love with Little Diver and asked her to be his wife. Since Little Diver thought it would be great fun to be Crane's wife and have him fish for her while she kept house and enjoyed herself in the company of other birds, she consented to marry him. Crane thought he and Little Diver would live happily together. He believed that she would continue to dive after fish in deep water, and he would continue to wade for fish in shallow water. This would allow them to always have a good supply of food.

Arrangements were quickly made for the wedding. Birds from far and wide were invited. After the marriage ceremony was over, a big dinner of many varieties of fish was served. On the morning following the wedding, Crane, as usual, went fishing. He only caught enough fish for himself, expecting his wife to catch her usual supply. Much to his surprise, his wife went swimming instead of fishing. Before Crane left home the next morning, she told him very plainly that it was the duty of a good husband to provide food for his family and that she did not feel it would be necessary for her to help him. Poor Crane had to fish twice as hard to catch enough for the two of them.

The following morning, Crane's wife told him that one of her relatives would be having dinner with them that evening. This meant that poor Crane had to wade in deeper water and work three times as hard as he had ever done before he was married. Worse still, his wife's relative did not leave after dinner. A few days later, another relative of his wife came to live with them. Crane said nothing about his increased responsibilities and instead worked harder and harder. In order to catch more fish, Crane had to fish in water so deep that he had to stand on his tiptoes while he was fishing. To make matters worse, his wife's relatives continued to arrive. They never helped him fish and greedily ate every morsel he caught.

To catch enough fish to feed such a big family, Crane needed to have longer legs so he could wade into deeper water. He began to lengthen his legs by pulling and stretching them as far as he could. As the days passed, Crane kept stretching his legs. They gradually became longer as well as more blue from wading in such cold water. Finally, there was no flesh left on his legs at all; they were nothing but long bones covered with scaly skin. Crane has never been able to wade out far enough to catch enough fish for his wife and her relatives. This is why, even today, Crane always has such a forlorn and worried look.

● ● ●

AH MO . . .

8

The Sun
and the Moon

A Snoqualmie Legend

A long time ago, two young Indian maidens were lying on their backs under the night sky. Just when the moon emerged from behind a large fir tree, they saw two stars fall. When the first star fell, the first maiden said, "That is your future husband coming for you."

When the next star fell, the other maiden said, "That is your future husband coming for you."

The girls were very excited and remained awake for a long time. Finally, after many hours, they went to sleep. When they awoke, they found they had spoken the truth about the falling stars. Each of them now had a husband who had taken them to the land of the star people while they slept.

The two men sent their wives out each day to dig for roots, and told them not to dig roots that were too deep or they might fall through the hole to the earth. After many moons had passed, both the young women became homesick. One day, as they dug up a very deep camas root, they pierced the floor of the sky and saw the earth. The women carefully covered up the opening and said nothing to their husbands.

Each day when the women went out to dig roots, they collected milkweeds. By twisting the weeds together, they were able to make a strong rope. The women gradually added twisted milkweeds to this rope until it was long enough to reach the earth.

The wives took so much time in making the rope that their husbands complained about not having enough roots to eat. This made the young wives even more anxious to leave. Early one morning, the two women tied the rope to a tree, enlarged the secret opening, and slid down to the earth.

A few months later, each of the young women had a baby boy. The two boys quickly became best friends. One day several years later, the mothers left the two boys with a friend while they went into the woods to pick berries. Before the mothers had returned, the fathers came down from the sky and took the two boys away. To punish their wives, the men then hid the children in a deep cave.

When the mothers returned from picking berries and found their children gone, they cried with grief. Fortunately, Blue Jay had seen the fathers take the children and told the young mothers where their sons were hidden. Blue Jay also told the women that the star people had used magic to cause the door of the cave to open and shut so as to crush any person who might try to enter.

The mothers begged Blue Jay to return their children to them. Blue Jay took pity on the mothers and agreed. The bird went to the door of the cave and looked inside. Just as he looked in, the door snapped shut. Blue Jay pulled back his head, but not in time to prevent it from being crushed very flat. You will notice this the next time you see a blue jay.

Blue Jay carefully watched how the door opened and closed. When the bird felt confident, he quickly rushed in just after the cave opened. Blue Jay moved a large rock into the path of the door so that it kept the door open, just long enough for him to take a boy in each hand and escape.

After they had become Indian braves, the more adventurous of the two men decided to find his father. While he tried and tried, he failed to find where his father lived. His anger made him rise into the sky where he turned into the Sun. He shone so hot that he burned nearly every person, plant, and animal on the earth. When the young man became tired of being the Sun, he came down from the sky and returned to his mother. Following his friend's example, the other young Indian brave decided to try to find his father. The second young man tried for many years but also failed. The young Indian brave was so upset that he also changed into the Sun, but he did not shine so strongly as to burn the earth. The other young Indian brave soon became lonely and decided to join his friend. This is why he became the Moon. To this day, the two young Indian braves make a daily trip around the earth.

• • •

9

Why the Robin Has a Red Breast

A Suquamish Legend

A long time ago, South Wind blew so hard and hot that many of the animals were very unhappy. Blue Jay scolded South Wind for making it uncomfortable for him even in the shade. Squirrel finally became so tired of the heat and Blue Jay's scolding that he called a council meeting to decide how to stop South Wind from annoying them. After much discussion, the animals decided to travel south until they found the home of South Wind.

After a long and hard journey, the animals learned that the source of South Wind was a fortress on top of a rocky mountain. Unfortunately, the sides of the mountain were too steep to climb. The animals tried and tried but could not reach the source of South Wind. Finally, by creeping up a small crack in the rocks, Mouse was able to reach the fortress.

Mouse was so small he was able to enter the fortress without being seen or heard. Once he was inside, Mouse learned that five brothers caused South Wind to blow. Mouse also saw that the brothers had many bows and arrows for defending the fortress. He quickly and quietly ate each of the bow strings. When the five brothers fell asleep that evening, Mouse made a long ladder of twisted milkweed and let it down so the other animals could climb up. When the five brothers saw that the animals were in the fortress, they ran for their bows and arrows. When the brothers discovered that their weapons were useless, they cried out in anger. After a short struggle, four of the brothers were captured by the animals. One brother managed to escape and was never seen again. To this day, the brother who was not caught continues to blow when he feels strong. But his wind seldom does any harm because his brothers cannot help him.

The animals were very happy. To celebrate, they burned the bows and arrows which they had captured from the five brothers. The animals had a grand time dancing around the fire. Only Robin refused to join the dancing. Instead, he stood quietly facing the fire. He remained there so long that his breast turned red. It remains this color even today.

• • •

AH MO . . .

10

The Coyote

A Kittitas Legend

A long time ago, the animals decided to climb to the land of the stars from the top of Huckleberry Mountain to find the secret of fire. When they arrived, they found two sisters who had been kidnapped by the star people. With the help of the sisters, the animals made a long rope of milkweed and thistle stalks and slid down to the earth. While each of the animals tried to bring fire with them, every spark went out except for one live coal which Beaver kept alive in his paw by fanning it with his big flat tail. The animals were very happy to have obtained fire to cook with and to keep them warm.

The fire was kept alive by the animals for a very long time. They covered it every night with ashes and kept careful watch to make sure that it did not go out. But after many moons had come and gone, the animals became careless. One morning when they got up and poked the ashes, they could not find a single spark.

The animals were very upset. Each blamed the others for letting the fire go out. They scolded and argued with each other until wise old Bull Frog said, "Why don't we select the best runners and ask them to run in the direction the wind blew? If they hurry, they may be able to catch the fire. I saw sparks blowing up toward Huckleberry Mountain before I went to sleep."

"So did I," added Beaver.

"Who can run the fastest?" asked Mole, who could not see at all.

Some animals believed Jack Rabbit was the fastest, while others believed it was Deer. In the hope he might be chosen to chase the fire, Coyote began showing off to the other animals. Coyote was sleek and muscular. The sun reflected off his smooth and glossy sides. He was sure that if anybody could catch the sparks from the fire, it would be him. Then, without waiting for the other animals to ask him, Coyote took off through the woods faster than the wind had ever blown. His big, bushy tail could hardly keep up with him. After he had run for many miles, Coyote became tired. Coyote's tongue hung out and the froth from his mouth covered his sides.

"Where are you going?" yelled Bear as Coyote ran past him.

"When are you coming back?" asked Hawk when he saw Coyote run by. Coyote did not answer and ran even faster.

"Perhaps he's running away," chirped Tree Toad to Hawk. Coyote still kept running.

Many hours later, Wildcat happened to be following the trail of Cougar. He hoped to find a deer his big brother had killed and left behind. Suddenly, he heard a faint noise. When Wildcat listened carefully, he heard Coyote gasp for breath. Wildcat walked toward the noise and saw Coyote.

"Why are you so tired?" asked Wildcat.

"I'm trying to catch up with the last sparks of fire," whispered Coyote, who was now only a shadow of his former self and was limping along on only three legs.

As soon as Wildcat learned what Coyote was after, he started to run after the sparks. Coyote, with his last bit of strength, caught Wildcat by the tail and held him back.

"Let go of my tail!" demanded Wildcat.

Coyote held on tight to the tail because he knew he was close to the sparks. Coyote wanted all the glory for himself.

"Let go of my tail!" demanded Wildcat again. Coyote shook his head and refused. Wildcat then saw a big spark of fire just ahead. Coyote saw it too, but he was too exhausted to run any further. He wound himself around a small tree and held on to Wildcat's tail with all his might. Wildcat struggled hard against Coyote. Finally, Wildcat was able to break free—but only by leaving his tail behind.

Wildcat caught up with the wind and snatched the spark of fire in his mouth. When the fire burned him, he wrinkled his nose and turned up his lips so he could place the spark between his front teeth. He then returned the fire to the other animals and was a hero.

Ever since that day, wildcats have had a bobtail and wrinkled nose. Coyotes have never recovered their good looks or their shining fur. To this day, they are as slim as a shadow.

• • •

11

The Fish Duck and the Sea Gull

A Skagit Legend

A long time ago, Sea Gull was a great diver and Fish Duck could not dive at all. Fish Duck decided that it was the narrow shape of her wishbone that caused Sea Gull to dive so well. Fish Duck, who was jealous of Sea Gull's diving, devised a plan. Fish Duck went out fishing and caught enough fish for a big dinner. He then invited Sea Gull to dine with him. Sea Gull accepted the invitation. She had to travel a long way to reach Fish Duck's home and was very hungry when she arrived. When the dinner hour came, Fish Duck had a wonderful meal for Sea Gull.

"How did you catch so many fish to eat?" asked Sea Gull.

"I dive for my fish," lied Fish Duck.

"How is it you can dive deep enough to get so many kinds of fish?" Sea Gull wanted to know.

"By having such a broad wishbone," answered Fish Duck, deceiving her still further.

After the meal was over, Fish Duck led his guest down to a nearby lake where Fish Duck, intending to impress Sea Gull, rested himself gracefully upon the water.

Sea Gull was jealous and asked, "What makes you sit so lightly on the water?"

"My broad wishbone allows me to sit on the water like a feather," lied Fish Duck.

Upon hearing this, Sea Gull, who was very vain, decided to obtain Fish Duck's wishbone through trickery.

"Let me try your wishbone and you try mine," suggested Sea Gull.

The two birds quickly exchanged wishbones, which was just what Fish Duck wanted.

To this day, the fish duck has a narrow wishbone and is a famous diver. The sea gull can sit gracefully upon the water, but cannot dive below the surface unless she falls quickly from the sky. Even then, the only fish the sea gull can catch are the small ones that swim near the surface.

• • •

AH MO . . .

12

The North Wind

A Snoqualmie Legend

A long time ago, North Wind lived on an island near the top of the world. North Wind blew so hard for so long that he blew away all the island plants and animals. The island was then nothing but rocks and gravel. After many moons had passed, North Wind became lonely and his disposition grew worse. Then he began to blow cold. He blew so hard and so cold in the spring that the flowers could not bloom and the grass could not grow in the neighboring lands. In the summer, his icy wind froze even the flowers and plants far to the south. In the fall, North Wind made life miserable for all the animals and food became scarce. In the winter, he made the snow come early and stay late.

The blowing wind caused great suffering for every animal. So the animals decided to hold a council meeting to plan how to stop North Wind. At the meeting, the animals decided to find the home of North Wind and stop him from blowing. Every animal was assigned a different job to prepare for the long trip. Eagle was selected as the chief scout. Swan ferried the small animals across the lakes and rivers. Beaver cut ferns and plants for their beds at night. Badger dug roots for food. Squirrel found pine nuts for dessert. Only Mole, who could not dig fast enough to keep up with the other animals, was left behind.

As the animals traveled north, the days grew shorter and the nights grew longer and colder.

Finally, the sun did not shine at all. Fortunately, the moon shone nearly all of the time and the stars were many times larger and brighter than they were at home. Some of the animals were afraid because there was no more daylight and wanted to turn back. Bear, for one, said it did not matter to him whether it was warm or cold. Every winter he covered himself with leaves in a hollow cedar stump and slept all winter. Sure enough, Bear did not show up for breakfast the next morning. Raven found him, sound asleep, between two big stones, and was not able to wake him. The other animals continued north without Bear.

The animals finally arrived at a beach near the top of the world. Just off the shore was the bare island where North Wind made his home. Whale lived in the water around this island. Because he was mischievious, Whale told North Wind that the animals were approaching and that they planned to make trouble for him. When North Wind saw the animals, he blew with all his might. The waves he made on the water rolled so high on the beach that there was hardly room for the animals to walk. The animals quickly made a shelter of logs and heavy stones to protect themselves from the storm.

The animals selected Eagle, who was brave and had powerful wings, to try to reach North Wind's home and capture him. Eagle tried with all his might but could not fly against the storm. Beaver then tried to swim through the water toward North

Wind. The huge waves quickly washed him back to shore. Porcupine, who had very short and stout legs, thought he could travel against the storm by staying close to the ground. He failed miserably and lost many of his precious quills.

After all the strong and clever animals had failed to move against the strong wind, Wren asked permission to try. All the animals laughed at Wren in spite of their own failures. Finally, Eagle said, "Go ahead and try little bird."

To the amazement of the other animals, Wren was so small that the rocks and pebbles on the bare island were big enough to shelter her from the wind; she dodged from one rock to another until she reached North Wind's house. Fortunately, North Wind hadn't seen Wren in the dust and snow blown up by his storm.

Wren found North Wind lying on his back and blowing through a window on the south side of his house. She carefully scouted around the house and found that, except for the window, it was sealed; she then began to peck at the string which held the window open. Her progress was slow but steady. When the string finally broke, the window slammed shut and stuck. North Wind was trapped in his own house.

The blowing stopped and the other animals quickly joined Wren. The animals then captured North Wind and tied him to two great logs which were frozen in the ground and served as headboard and footboard for his bed.

The animals were very happy they had captured the one who had ruined their land with his wind, and Wren was a heroine. Some animals wanted to kill North Wind and fill his house with snow. Other animals wanted to throw him in the cold water and let Walrus spear him with his long tusks. The animals could not agree on what to do with mean North Wind. Finally, Mud Hen said, "Wren caught him. Why not let her decide how to dispose of North Wind?"

All the animals agreed.

Wren told North Wind his life would be spared if he made three promises. First, he must never blow his cold breath again in the spring and summer in a way which would distress the animals or harm the trees, grass, or flowers. Second, he must never blow too cold on the North Pacific coast so the animals could always walk on the beach, even in winter. Third, he must promise that before the sun sets on summer evenings, he would blow cool air along the North Pacific coast so everyone could enjoy a good night's rest. North Wind quickly agreed. To this day on the North Pacific coast, you will never find snow on the beach in the winter or cold winds in spring and summer. You can also feel North Wind's cool breath on summer evenings.

• • •

AH MO ...

13

How the Indians Obtained Fire

A Snoqualmie Legend

A long time ago, the animals held a contest to decide who could shoot an arrow the greatest distance. While the competition was going on, a very small boy was making arrows nearby. He was using great care and he showed great skill. Coyote saw the boy and asked him why he was making arrows even though he was too weak to draw a bow. The boy quickly became angry and challenged Coyote to a contest. Coyote's sides shook with laughter when he heard the boy's challenge. After Coyote finished making fun of the boy, he accepted and said, "You shoot at a target I choose and I will shoot at any target you choose."

"You must shoot at a mosquito," replied the boy.

Coyote slowly prepared his bow and took careful aim at a passing mosquito. The arrow traveled swiftly but missed the target. Coyote was angry and decided to cheat. While Coyote was retrieving his arrow, he caught a mosquito in his paw and placed it on the point of his arrow. When Coyote returned to the boy, he pretended that the arrow had hit the target. Coyote then said to the boy, "Your target is the bright star shining through the tree tops."

The boy nodded to accept the challenge. He prepared his bow and walked to an opening between the branches of a large tree. After taking very careful aim, he shot his arrow. It flew so far and so accurately that it struck the bright star.

Coyote and the other animals were amazed by the boy's success. While the other animals were chattering about the boy's spectacular feat, Spider, who had been living on the star, began to spin a fine web, which soon reached from the boy's arrow to the ground. When he finished the web and landed on the earth, the animals knew that Spider was the boy's guardian spirit and that it was he who had guided the arrow to the star.

The animals then climbed up Spider's web to the land of the star people. Every animal had been warned by Spider to keep quiet so they would not be discovered by the star people. The animals were surprised to see the star people using fire to warm themselves and to cook their food. When the star people were asleep, the animals slowly approached the fire. Jack Rabbit stood up and warmed his feet and Kingfisher flew around the fire and dried his feathers. Then the other animals began to dance around the fire. Beaver was the only animal who did not join the dancing. Instead, Beaver slipped away, hid himself in a fish trap, and waited.

When the star people finally woke up and saw the animals dancing around the fire, they ran to catch them. Each of the animals hastily grabbed a spark from the fire and scampered down Spider's web to the earth. Unfortunately, by the time they reached the earth, every spark of fire had gone out.

While the animals were feeling sorry about the loss of the fire, Beaver suddenly struck the earth with a great thump! Beaver did not move or breathe for many minutes. While the animals were trying to revive Beaver, they opened his paws and found he was holding a spark from the fire. Beaver had cleverly waited until the star people were distracted before grabbing the spark. Unfortunately, he had tried to climb down the web by using only one paw, and he had slipped and fallen. This is why Beaver struck the ground with such a thump and why his fire did not go out.

Beaver's guardian spirit saw that he had lost his breath and felt sorry for him. The guardian spirit quickly appeared in the form of an otter and stepped over Beaver three times. Minutes later, Beaver came back to life and was honored by the other animals for having brought fire to the earth.

● ● ●

Judge
Arthur E. Griffin

Arthur Eugene Griffin was born April 1, 1862, in New Haven Township, Olmstead County, Minnesota, the son of Lorenzo and Julia Griffin. His early childhood was spent on his father's farm in a sparsely settled part of Olmstead County, where the family lived in a log house with hewn logs for a floor. Arthur received his early education in the simple one-room schools of the district. After finishing school in Minnesota, he worked for a railroad and saved enough money to move to Chicago.

After graduating from a business school, he took a job as a cook with a Canadian Pacific Railway survey crew. In 1884, Arthur arrived in Tacoma on an inspection trip. He liked Washington State so much that he quit his job with the railroad and began to work in the hop fields of Ezra Meeker. A few months later, he began teaching school at Alderton in Pierce County, a job he was offered because of his penmanship.

When the Northern Pacific Railroad passed through land well suited for a town, Arthur moved from Alderton and became one of the area's earliest merchants. The town was later named Enumclaw. Having had some experience in a Minnesota hardware store, he and his partner, John Blake, opened a general store on what is now Griffin Avenue opposite the Lee Hotel. Arthur was Enumclaw's first postmaster and justice of the peace. Mr. Blake was the first mayor. While working at his store, Arthur heard about a beautiful French girl who was teaching school nearby. Following a spirited courtship, Arthur married Gabrielle Paumell in May, 1889, the same year Washington became a state. His bride's father was one of the earliest settlers of the Green River Valley.

While living in Enumclaw, Arthur began to prepare himself for entering the legal profession. The town wanted to incorporate and asked him to prepare the necessary documents. He studied law by taking a course prepared by the territory's Representative-at-Large in the United States Congress.

After Arthur was admitted to practice law in 1890, he and his wife moved to Seattle and built a home on a view lot on Queen Anne Hill. Only two houses stood between their house and what today is the ship canal. Because of its exposed location, the first house was firmly bolted to a large stump. The stump was the home of large black ants, which Gabrielle fought for many years with a saucer of powdered sugar and borax. After dinner, if weather permitted, Arthur and Gabrielle combed Queen Anne Hill for the glacial grandiorite boulders which would be used in the foundations and walls of their second house. The design for the house was copied from a wing of a Los Angeles mansion. Every stone was dressed by Italian masons. It is a good example of what the irreverent call "Seattle's granite mausoleums." The house still stands at 1224 First North.

In 1897, like many Seattle residents, Arthur went to Alaska during the great "Gold Rush." In addition to practicing law, he prospected and mined for a year. Whenever Arthur received news of a large gold strike, the law office was promptly closed. Arthur found several claims, but they were jumped by other prospectors. One day he visited the claim of a man who owed him money. He was told to scoop up some gold as payment of the debt. These were the only nuggets he later brought home to Seattle.

Arthur returned from Alaska after three years and was elected to serve as a judge of the Superior Court of King County. His career as a judge was marked by many able decisions. He resumed private legal practice in 1910 so he could form a partnership with his son, Arthur R. Griffin. The two men practiced law for many years under the name Griffin & Griffin.

In his private practice, Judge Griffin was a passionate advocate of justice for Indians in the State of Washington. Mrs. LaClaire of the Yakima Indian reservation had a sleeping porch added for his frequent visits. Judge Griffin's entire family would often journey to Indian reservations by car. Staying in a smoke-scented tepee was always enjoyable for the judge. The tents were very clean because the Indians were continually bathing and fanning dirt from the sides of the tepee, which were raised just enough for perfect ventilation. Canning was done by a stream in the shade. The judge once obtained an Indian's signature by dipping his thumb in wild huckleberry juice from a canning kettle.

In his time, Washington State certainly had no greater authority on Indian law. One of his cases was heard by the U.S. Supreme Court. Judge Griffin was seldom financially rewarded for his efforts to defend Indian rights. Instead, the Indians paid him with friendship, beautiful stories, and small presents. For many years, the Judge had particularly coveted a superbly carved, nephrite jade ax. The Indians teasingly kept the ax from him until it suited their purpose. When they finally gave the ax to Judge Griffin, they also gave him the nickname "Old Stone Ax."

Judge Griffin was a businessman as well as a lawyer. He had several investments in Mexico as well as a ranch located near Olympia, Washington. The sheep he kept on the ranch earned him a fortune when the price of wool soared during World War I. While the ranch was eventually sold, one five-acre tract was donated for the construction of a school. The Griffin Elementary School, located west of Olympia on the Shelton Highway, was built on this land.

On December 26, 1947, Judge Griffin was struck and killed by a car at the age of eighty-five. His friends and admirers came to the Mountain View Cemetery, chosen for its view, to pay their last respects. May the moon shine on Mount Rainier for Old Stone Ax to admire.

Museums with Significant Collections of Northwest Indian Culture

1. Thomas Burke Memorial Washington State Museum, University of Washington, Seattle, Washington.
2. Washington State Historical Society, Tacoma, Washington.
3. Portland Art Museum, Portland, Oregon.
4. Campbell River and District Museum, Campbell River, British Columbia, Canada.
5. Queen Charlotte Islands Museum, Skidegate, Canada.
6. University of British Columbia Museum of Anthropology, Vancouver, British Columbia, Canada.
7. Royal British Columbia Museum, Victoria, British Columbia, Canada.
8. Anchorage Museum of History and Art, Anchorage, Alaska.
9. American Museum of Natural History, New York, New York.
10. Museum of the American Indian, Heye Foundation, New York, New York.
11. Princeton University Museum of Natural History, Princeton, New Jersey.

More Ah Mo

Indian Legends from the Northwest

Compiled by Judge Arthur Griffin
Edited by Trenholme J. Griffin
ISBN 0-88839-303-2
5.5" x 8.5" • sc • 64 pages

MORE AH MO

Indian Legends from the Northwest

Compiled by Judge Arthur Griffin
Edited by Trenholme J. Griffin

63

Suggested Reading List

Ashwell, Reg. *Coast Salish: Their Art, Culture and Legends*. Surrey: Hancock House Publishers Ltd. 1978.

Ashwell, Reg. *Indian Tribes of the Northwest*. Surrey: Hancock House Publishers Ltd. 1977.

Batdorf, Carol. *Northwest Native Harvest*. Surrey: Hancock House Publishers Ltd. 1990.

Batdorf, Carol. *Power Quest*. Surrey: Hancock House Publishers Ltd. 1990.

Batdorf, Carol. *Spirit Quest*. Surrey: Hancock House Publishers Ltd. 1990.

Drew, Leslie, and Wilson, Douglas. *Argillite: Art of the Haida*. Surrey: Hancock House Publishers Ltd. 1980.

George, Chief Dan. *My Heart Soars*. Surrey: Hancock House Publishers Ltd. 1974.

George, Chief Dan. *My Spirit Soars*. Surrey: Hancock House Publishers Ltd. 1982.

Goddard, P. E., and Kew, Della. *Indian Art and Culture of the Northwest Coast*. Surrey: Hancock House Publishers Ltd. 1974.

Hirnschall, Helmut. *The Song of Creation: North American Indian Myths and Original Paintings*. Surrey: Hancock House Publishers Ltd. 1979.

Kaiper, Dan and Nancy. *Tlingit: Their Art, Culture and Legends*. Surrey: Hancock House Publishers Ltd. 1978.

Smyly, John and Carolyn. *Those Born at Koona: The Totem Poles of the Haida Village Skedans, Queen Charlotte Islands*. Surrey: Hancock House Publishers Ltd. 1973.

Wallas, James, and Whitaker, Pamela. *Kwakiutl Legends*. Surrey: Hancock House Publishers Ltd. 1989.

We-gyet Wanders On: Legends of the Northwest. Surrey: Hancock House Publishers Ltd. 1977.

ISBN 0-88839-244-3 $5.95

AH MO

Indians Legends from the Northwest
Edited by Tren J. Griffin

hancock

house

Tren J. Griffin

"The *Ah Mo* Indian leg
ends flow with the spirit o
nature. They are delightfu
stories, as unique as the win
and weather of the North
west, and are certain to spar
the imagination of both chil
and adult."

—*Joel Pritchar*
Lieutenant Governo
Washington Stat

These never-before-published legends were collected by pic
neer merchant and attorney Judge Arthur E. Griffin, beginning i
1884. They have been passed down through five generations of th
Griffin family, and now have been edited for publication by Tren
holme J. Griffin. The great-grandson of the judge, Trenholme i
steeped in the treasury of these delightful stories, and deftly applie
the storyteller's free-flowing style.

Mr. Griffin is a Seattle-based attorney with a practice emphasiz
ing international commercial transactions. He has published *Korea*
The Tiger Economy, Taiwan: Re
public of China, The Korea Guide
book, 1989, and *The Global Nego*
tiator, 1.990.

The *Ah Mo* legends make idea
bedtime stories for children o
pleasure-time reading for adults.

ISBN 0-88839-244-3

50000

EAN

9 780888 392442

CHRISTOPHER J. H. WRIGHT

TO THE

CROSS

PROCLAIMING *the* GOSPEL *from*
the UPPER ROOM *to* CALVARY